UNGLE
ABIES
the Amazon
Rain Forest

South American Tapirs

by Rachel Lynette

Consultant:
Dr. Mark C. Andersen
Department of Fish, Wildlife and Conservation Ecology
New Mexico State University

BEARPORT
PUBLISHING
New York, New York

Credits

Cover and Title, © Minden Pictures/SuperStock; 4–5, 22 (middle), © Tamara Kulikova/ Shutterstock Images; 6, © Red Line Editorial; 6–7, 22 (top), © Colin Edwards Photography/ Shutterstock Images; 8–9, 22 (bottom), © Micha Klootwijk/Shutterstock Images; 9, © Red Line Editorial; 10–11, © Pete Oxford/naturepl.com; 12, 23 (bottom), © Pilar Echevarria/ Shutterstock Images; 12–13, © Tier und Naturfotografie/SuperStock; 14, 23 (top), © Naaman Abreu/Shutterstock Images; 14–15, © Gerard Lacz Images/SuperStock; 16–17, © age fotostock/SuperStock; 18–19, © Minden Pictures/SuperStock; 20–21, © Minden Pictures/SuperStock; 23 (middle), © AND Inc./Shutterstock Images.

Publisher: Kenn Goin
Editor: Joy Bean
Creative Director: Spencer Brinker
Photo Researcher: Arnold Ringstad
Design: Emily Love

Library of Congress Cataloging-in-Publication Data

Lynette, Rachel.
   South American tapirs / by Rachel Lynette.
      pages cm. — (Jungle babies of the Amazon rain forest)
   Includes bibliographical references and index.
   Audience: Ages 6-9.
   ISBN-13: 978-1-61772-759-7 (library binding)
   ISBN-10: 1-61772-759-8 (library binding)
   1. Tapirs—South America—Juvenile literature. I. Title.
   QL737.U64L96 2013
   599.66—dc23

                                2012039864

For more information, write to Bearport Publishing Company, Inc., 45 West 21st Street, Suite 3B, New York, New York 10010. Printed in the United States of America.

10 9 8 7 6 5 4 3 2

Contents

Meet a tapir calf

In a grassy area by a lake, a mother tapir and her **calf** rest.

It is the middle of the day, but they are sleepy.

4

The mother and calf were awake
all night searching for food.

mother
tapir

calf

What is a tapir?

A tapir is a **mammal** with a long, bendable nose, or snout.

Adult tapirs are very large—they can weigh up to 700 pounds (318 kg).

They have brown or red fur and a short **mane** on their heads and necks.

Tapir calves have white stripes and dots on their fur when they are born.

Adult South American tapir size

Although they do have a mane like their parents, it's much shorter.

mane

white stripes

dots

Where do tapirs live?

South American tapirs live near lakes, rivers, and swamps in **rain forests**.

Some other kinds of tapirs, however, live high in mountain forests.

No matter where they live, most tapirs spend time near water because they like to swim.

tapir swimming

☐ **Where South American tapirs live**

North America

Atlantic Ocean

Central America

South America

Pacific Ocean

N
W E
S

At home in the water

Tapir calves can swim when they are just a few days old.

The water keeps them cool and washes insects from their bodies.

When they are afraid, the calves go underwater to hide.

They can hold their breath for several minutes.

A special snout

A tapir uses its long nose to sniff out fruit and other plant foods.

It also uses it to grab hold of things such as branches.

To breathe underwater, the tapir uses its snout like a **snorkel**.

snorkel being used by a person

tapir sniffing around for food

snout

Giving birth

A mother tapir has just one calf at a time.

When she is ready to give birth, she finds a safe, hidden spot on land.

She does not want **predators**, such as jaguars and crocodiles, to find her newborn calf.

crocodile

Blending in

A mother tapir sometimes leaves her new calf alone while she looks for food.

However, she expects that her calf will be safe by itself.

new calf

The calf's white stripes help it blend in with the rain forest's many colors.

This makes it hard for predators to spot the baby tapir.

mother

Finding food

At one week old, the calf starts following its mother when she looks for food.

The pair usually search for food at night.

The calf learns which plants to eat by watching its mother.

Tapirs eat many different kinds of plants, such as grasses, tree leaves, and fruits.

Bananas are one of their favorite foods.

tapir eating leaves

19

All grown up

By the time it is seven months old, a tapir calf's stripes have faded.

It is not a full-grown adult, however, until it is 18 months old.

Once they are adults, male tapirs usually live alone their entire lives.

Adult females only live alone until they have babies.

When the females are three years old, they are ready to start their own family.

Glossary

calf (KAF)
the baby of an animal
such as a tapir

mammal (MAM-uhl)
a warm-blooded
animal that has hair
and drinks its mother's
milk as a baby

mane (MANE)
a growth of stiff hair
on the head and
neck of some animals

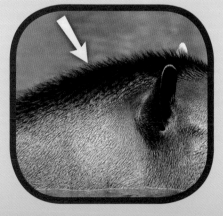

predators (PRED-uh-turz) animals that hunt and eat other animals

rain forests (RAYN FOR-ists) large, warm areas of land covered with trees and plants, where lots of rain falls

snorkel (SNOR-kuhl) an air tube that is used for breathing underwater

Index

Read more

Franklin, Carolyn. *Rain Forest Animals (World of Wonder).* New York: Scholastic (2008).

Kalman, Bobbie. *Baby Animals in Rain Forest Habitats (Habitats of Baby Animals).* New York: Crabtree Publishing (2012).

Learn more online

To learn more about South American tapirs, visit
www.bearportpublishing.com/JungleBabies

About the author

Rachel Lynette has written more than 100 nonfiction books for children. She also creates resources for teachers. Rachel lives near Seattle, Washington. She enjoys biking, hiking, crocheting hats, and spending time with her family and friends.